FINDING GLOCCA MORA

a home left behind

FINDING GLOCCA MORA

a home left behind

T. GILDEA-SOLOMOS

StoryTerrace

Text Marguerite O'Callaghan
Copyright © T. GILDEA-SOLOMOS

First print August 2023

StoryTerrace

www.StoryTerrace.com

CONTENTS

FRONTISPIECE	9
PREFACE	11
1: CHILD OF THE DIASPORA	17
2: IMMIGRANTS LIVE AND DIE AWAY FROM HOME	27
3: I AM AN UNRELENTING FENIAN BASTARD	31
4: IRISH GRANDMA MAGIC	37
5: GRANDMA TAKES THE LEAD	43
6: LESSONS IN IRISH HISTORY	55
7: WHY MOM LEFT IRELAND	65
8: I WISH I WERE BACK HOME IN DERRY	69
9: IRELAND IS CLOSED FOR BUSINESS	77
10: A SAFE LANDING	89

11: SHOULD I STAY OR SHOULD I GO?   101

12: ARRIVAL   111

FRONTISPIECE

I hear a bird.
Is it a Derry bird?
It well may be, he's bringin' me,
A cheerin' word.

I feel a breeze.
A River Shannon breeze.
It well may be, she's followed me,
Across the seas...
Then tell me, please,
How are things in Glocca Mora?

FINIAN'S RAINBOW

The river, at Carrick on Shannon

PREFACE

Bronx Irish Catholic - that was my identity growing up in New York City. Those of us who shared that moniker would ask, "What Parish do you live in?" instead of the typical "What part of the city do you live in?". The Parish was our community, our village, or our town.

It has been 50 years since I lived in Manhattan and the Bronx. But just a few months ago, when meeting another American, from NYC, who was first-generation Irish born, I asked him what Parish he was from, and with a big grin he declared, Good Shepherd Parish, and I knew immediately he was from the Inwood neighborhood.

Mom and Dad had emigrated from Ireland in 1929-1930. They escaped as teenagers from the political upheaval of the Irish War of Independence, the Irish Civil War, and the creation of both a Republic - with 26 counties - and a Northern Irish Commonwealth in the remaining 6 counties of what once was Ulster, Ireland.

My parents traded those troubles for the challenge of finding employment in the United States, at the height of the Great American Depression. And they succeeded.

Surviving that, they next struggled through World War II.

When peacetime arrived, everyone was trying to recover from the financial losses and hard times of the previous decade. My Dad almost died of Meningitis, for lack of antibiotics on the homefront, and the grocery business they had built up, did succumb to Bankruptcy.

After 20 years of hard work in America, my parents were starting all over again financially. A situation that did not lend itself to telling their children stories about Irish history, heritage, or culture. As my Dad would say, it was all he could do "to keep the wolf from the door".

In 1950, my parents were both 40 years old when they were surprised by another birth: me. By now, Mom was no longer a housewife, but worked 40 hours a week, just like Dad. I guess we were poor. I know we lived from one paycheck to the next; each one went to rent, utilities, and school tuition as soon as it was received.

Every one of us worked to keep our home neat and clean and we laughed every day, at each other and at ourselves. Life was good - rich with caring, believing, church community, a sense of belonging, and happiness in our family unit. We worked together towards common goals; financial, educational, and professional.

My siblings came of age, got jobs, had weddings, and had babies.

I came of age, became a nurse, and eloped with my boyfriend, who recently returned from Vietnam. Our marriage lasted only 5 1/2 years.

Then, I had a proper wedding, to my Greek husband. We were both children who were first-generation Americans. As kids of immigrants we shared common goals when we met and married: to have children, own a home, care for our parents, and create a family. Our marriage lasted 32 years and produced 3 terrific human beings, each one with a quick wit, good looks, and a strong work ethic. By 2010, those goals had been accomplished, and with little left in common, we divorced.

Two years later, thanks to online dating, "Chet" was now living with me. He was a real character: an unusually tall (6ft 7in) Orthodox Jew, from Texas, whose hobby was collecting muskets from the American Civil War era. An experienced gun-smith, he kept each one in pristine order and we would shoot with them at various events.

During one such trip to San Antonio, several of his friends were excited to find that I was 100% Irish. Apparently, 'The Role of the Irish in the American Civil War' had been the topic of one guy's Masters Degree, and he amazed me with stories and facts.

This was when I discovered the magic and wonder of the Irish people and their role in world history. I wanted to know it all. My pride knew no bounds and my excitement grew. Although I was in my 60s, it became imperative that I get my Irish passport, go to Ireland, learn why and how my parents left, and that I meet the family they left behind; my family.

A plan came into being:

- Retire. Sell the house and put furnishings in storage.
- Live in Ireland for 6 months to 1 year.
- Travel around Ireland with 1st cousins who were also widowed/divorced, and retired.
- Have my children visit and learn about their heritage.

- Return home, become a full-time Grandma, tell stories, and plan trips back to Ireland.

But that is not what happened.

This book is that story: what I did, where I went, who I met, and what I discovered. I know it surprised me. I hope you enjoy it.

The Gildeas in the Bronx - John, Ann, Terry, Jim, James Gildea and Mary Donnelly-Gildea circa 1976

1: CHILD OF THE DIASPORA

I am the child of immigrants. Irish immigrants.

At the start of the 20th century, Ireland was a land of farms without mechanized farm equipment. You worked the field with a horse-drawn plough, and you traveled by donkey and cart, not by car. That was the country my parents left behind in 1929-30.

Electric light was available in the city, day and night, but out on a farm, the dark of night was as cold and black as a pint of Guinness. Young and old alike were happiest and safest beside the peat fire on the hearth, in the company of loved ones. For it was the faeries and the spirits that traveled in the night, and you could never be sure what mood they would be in, should your path cross theirs. Now, to be sure, that is not the Ireland of today, nor has it been for many decades. But that was the Ireland my parents remembered.

We were raised on their tales of magic and wonder. How, walking home on a dark night you could meet a sorrowful ghost, begging for prayers of salvation or - God Forbid! - the D'vil himself might jump out of a hedge and follow you until you could find a river or stream to cross, so as to lose him!

I remember there was a Broadway Musical, called Finian's Rainbow, and it had a hit song playing on the radio, "How Are Things In Glocca Morra?" The opening lines referenced a Derry bird and a Shannon breeze. Because my mother was from Derry, and the River Shannon ran through my father's county, I learned all the words and sang them often to feel connected to the places my parents called home.

Although my college degree is in the sciences, it is outweighed by 12 years of Catholic education and this heritage of mysticism, thereby making me a true believer in every possibility: angels, spirits, other worlds, past lives, etc. No surprise then, that when my niece recommended a "legit" psychic, I booked a session.

This woman did prove herself to be gifted. "Bring actual photos of your family members, not the ones on your phone" were her instructions. Going through the photo albums, it was not easy to pull photos that didn't include my in-laws, Dottie and Bill, as they were an integral part of our children's lives. But I did find a group that was representative of my family now, "post-divorce".

This woman would hold each person's photo and after gazing at it for a few seconds, would give me a quick summary: "Your daughter loves you very much... your sons are protective of you... I see you with a lot of books, like a library."

None of this was exactly revelatory so you can imagine my shock when this woman, while holding a picture of my mother, lowered her head, looked away, sighed deeply, and asked, " WHO is Dottie?" And there is a man with her... Bill... She won't let anyone speak!"

All I could blurt out was, "My mother-in-law??? But I divorced…"

"Yes... she is telling me that the divorce doesn't matter, she wants you to know that she and Bill are with you often, and with your children, and they love and protect you."

This was not possible. Dottie and I were cordial but never friendly; same goes for Bill. How did this woman connect with them? Her response was funny: "I didn't connect with them! She interrupted me!"

This was beyond any parlor game trick. This lady obviously had a gift, so when she told me later that my Grandmother, Anne Walpole, is my Spirit Guide, I accepted this as truth. "Do you know a woman named Ann or Anna? Dark hair, she tells me she lives in a small house with lots of people coming and going, but it is just the way things are. She is happy with it. And she is with you always. Your guide."

"I had a grandmother named Anna..or Ann. I never met her. My father's mother."

"Yes... she is nodding. This is who she is."

My father's mother died ten years before I was born. My father had no photos of her, and he only spoke of her to me once. It was a pouring rainy day, and I came through the front door with a scarf tied beneath my chin when I heard Dad gasp. Turning, I looked directly at him.

"Holy Christ!" he whispered, staring at me. "Terry, I thought you were my mother walking through that door. You're the image of her!"

Shaking his head, and with a deep breath, he went off to make his cup of tea.

Nothing more was ever said, but for me, it was a golden moment - a link - to a family I never met but somehow always missed.

When I finally visited the home-place (now just a derelict building surrounded by overgrown brambles and rushes), I thought of my grandmother. This was a three-room cottage, better than some others. I thought that with seven children, two parents, and frequent visits from neighbors, there most certainly would have been a lot of coming and going.

As I walked from room to room, I imagined softly glowing peat burning in the side room fireplaces where the family slept. In the central room, I could imagine a roaring fire with a kettle suspended over it as my grandmother rocked and crooned to soothe a fussy baby in her arms. It felt welcoming and safe. I could picture my father, as a young boy, chasing about in the fields behind the house, and then as a young man, watching angry and confused as his brothers left home, only to be forced to do the same himself, four years later.

Touching the framework of the front door, I could see my grandmother kissing her boy goodbye, smoothing the front of his jacket, and telling him to be proud, to be good, and to come back if ever he could.

I couldn't have that kind of experience at my mom's home, in Quilly, because the family still lived there, but one of the cousins took me to a psychic she trusted.

Again, it was a little weird. Although she didn't pick up on my grandmother, she pulled out three decks of tarot and angel cards and said St Michael kept coming through - to tell me that I am "Sovereign" in Ireland and belong here.

"What does that mean?" I asked.

"It means this is your home; It means you're meant to be here."

This threw me for a loop since I had plans to leave within a few months. I blew it off, telling myself it was just another way of recognizing that my DNA is 100% Irish.

Dad as a young man, ploughing a field at his home, Corlaskagh, Leitrim

The Donnelly Children, 1929 Hugh, Henry, Gerry, Leonard and Leo with Mary (Mamie) & Teresa at the farm in Quilly, Derry

Mom and Dad. They were engaged to marry circa 1937. Dad's black armband is for his brother, Thom Pat

Mary Murphy-Donnelly and Joseph Donnelly, of Quilly, County Derry

Opposite: Ann Walpole-Gildea and John Gildea at their home in Corlaskagh, County Leitrim

2: IMMIGRANTS LIVE AND DIE AWAY FROM HOME

Dad was 19 years old when he arrived in Manhattan and the Bronx. He came to the care of two older brothers - Thomas Patrick and Francis - and began work in the grocery business.

Within six years, Thom Pat died from a type of influenza, leaving behind a pregnant wife and two little girls and leaving Frank as Dad's only immediate family in America. Sadly, Dad and Frank did not get along and were never close. Frank married young, and his six children were older than us – Dad's four children - by five to ten years, so we had little in common There were never any Gildea family get-togethers or visits at Christmas or any other holidays. Instead, Dad remained close with those friends and cousins he had gone to school with from back home who had also immigrated. These were the people we called Auntie and Uncle and claimed their kids as our first cousins.

Mom's story is so completely different you'd think she came from a different country. Oh wait - she did!

Born in Derry, Northern Ireland, she was a 'Royal British Subject' with a British passport. Mom came to an uncle she had never met, and who was told he would recognize her by the outfit she wore.

FINDING GLOCCA MORA

Imagine, on the docks of New York harbor, hundreds of people milling about, disembarking from a huge ship, and my mother standing there with her red ribbons in her hair so that her uncle will know her, and a man approaches;
"Are you Mary Donnelly?"
"Yes, sir, I am."
"Alright then, get in my car. I'm your uncle."
YIKES !

Her uncle, Harry Murphy, had his own family and could not afford to take her in. Within days of her arrival, she was brought to an agency to apply for work as Domestic Help. In October 1930, in America's Great Depression, Mom was 20 years of age, and if she wanted to keep a roof over her head and food on her plate, she had best keep her employers happy. It would be six years or more before Mom met and married Dad and created her own home. But she never stopped longing for the home she left behind.

Eighty years later...
Mom's little brother, Henry, inherited the farm and the house she grew up in. Now his granddaughter, Tracy, lived in Rhode Island in the States. As much as that farm was the home my mother left behind, it was also the home that Tracy left behind. Like Mom, Tracy knew that farm inside and out, from spending weekends and school holidays with her grandparents.

As a teenager, Tracy came to the States as a Nanny. She eventually met a guy, married and stayed, and Mom was her closest family. It was odd to see a 30-something Tracy, spending weekends, chatting for hours, in the Senior housing apartment with my 80-something mother. But they shared homesickness for the same place: the cottage, rose bush, high field, and cows. Now they shared boxes of Kleenex as they laughed and cried together. Mom was 92 when she died, and Tracy and her husband stayed with me for her funeral.

I lived in New Jersey. After my divorce, Tracy and I developed a closer relationship, having hour-long chats by telephone and the occasional visit for a weekend. During one of my stays, I learned things about my mother I never knew.

It seems that my mother never intended to leave Ireland. Neither did the family have the money to send her. My granddad had to sell the family cow to pay for her boat ticket. And none of her siblings followed. Everyone remained in Derry, got married, had careers and raised families.

Why did she leave? And if the money she sent from America wasn't an absolute necessity, why didn't she go back home?

Everyone alive at that time is now dead. The answer could be in old family stories and the social history of the time, but I would need to be in Ireland for quite a while to dig deep enough.

And so a seed was planted in my brain.

Mom and Dad both came to America by boat. Dad left from Cobh Harbor, Co. Cork. Mom left from Belfast Harbor, Co. Antrim

This is what is left of the pier where so many boarded ships to America and Canada. Cobh is known as the Harbor of Tears

3: I AM AN UNRELENTING FENIAN BASTARD

After my divorce, I had a Gentleman friend named Chet, who was 6ft 7 in, and a Texas Democrat. He was also an Orthodox Jew and a Civil War Aficionado. We met online, and he lived with me for 2.5 years. Following a 32-year marriage, comprised of raising three children, teaching Sunday School, caring for elderly parents, working full time as a Nurse and having a husband who didn't like to take vacations......Chet was a Lot of Fun!

His life was so far removed from what I had been living. A Viet Nam Vet, he had served in the artillery and emerged with a love of big guns. Actually - all types of guns. As a part-time gunsmith and collector, his pride was his series of muskets from 1860 through 1867, which he maintained in full working order, along with an assortment of other muskets and smaller handguns and pistols. Bill Kennedy, the gunsmith who created Johnny Depp's pistols for 'The Pirates of the Caribbean', was a close friend and taught Chet much of what he knew. He maintained three cannons, owned by 2 of his buddies, which we took to Civil War events. Chet would briefly lecture about the cannons and cannon balls, and we would fire one off! Over the course of our 3-year relationship, I attended many of these historical weekend events in Key West, Pennsylvania, Texas, and the Carolinas, where he had friends and associates who had written their degree treatises on different aspects of the Civil War. But what sticks with me to this day is what I learned from these individuals about "…..the role of the Irish in the American Civil War..." and how that spurred me to learn more about my heritage and history.

That was eight years ago, and friends still laugh, asking me, "How did you EVER hook up with that guy Chet?? You two were so different." And they're right. But, remember my Grandma Ann - my spirit guide? I believe she made it happen because it brought me to my Irish origins.

The history of Irish rebellions, and uprisings, is a rabbit hole that I fell into head first. I would regale co-workers with the story about the Fenians invading Canada. This is a great story about Irish veterans of the American Civil War. Having survived the war and coming from the Union and Confederate armies, they hatched a plan to take Canada hostage. Outfitted by Irish American Donors and the American Government, they had their own "Designer" green uniforms with gold shamrock epaulets. With all the supplies, pack mules, cannons and muskets they could carry, they marched North to seize Canada from the British. Once it was under their control, they would demand Ireland's independence in exchange for Canada's return.

It was a failed attempt. The only consequence of their action was that Canada then created a Legal Border. I don't think the Fenians realized the true size of Canada.! Their Moxy was admirable, even if their lack of intel was woeful.

This Fenian group evolved into the Irish Volunteers, who orchestrated the 1916 Uprising. When the uprising leaders were summarily executed - after WW I had just been fought for the right of all small nations to their own independence - Britain's hypocrisy was noted, and civilized nations were outraged.

My visceral reaction to all of this information was feelings of deja -vu. I believe I lived previous lives as a Fenian and later as a Volunteer. Or, could it be that I wanted so much to be part of it? It was no longer enough to know general history. I wanted to know my family history, our story, our bloodline.

The next step was a DNA test with Ancestry.com.

My dad was what they call "Black Irish": thick black hair, piercing blue eyes, and skin that would turn olive in summer. My mom was blue-eyed too, with dark wavy hair, but her father was ginger, as were many of his grandchildren. I began hoping for some Spanish Armada or Viking marauder blood in my genetic DNA material.

Nope. I was 100% Irish, all from the island's Northern part. OK, no real surprise there. My parents were probably the first generation in their entire ancestry to leave the island. But I had raised my children in the Greek Orthodox faith and with predominantly Greek traditions for every holiday. My children identified as American, of Greek culture, with some Irish. The fault is mine, but I made the best choice I could.

When we married, I had to decide whether to insist on a Roman Catholic wedding, resulting in my husband's excommunication from his church, or agree to a Greek Orthodox wedding - resulting in my Mother not attending.

When I consulted a monsignor at St.Patrick's Cathedral in Manhattan, I was recommended to have a Greek-Orthodox wedding. Seeing the surprise on my face, he explained that, following Vatican II, all sacraments in the Greek Orthodox Church are accepted as valid by the Roman Catholic Church. But that the Greek Orthodox Church did not recognize any other church and would excommunicate any followers who participated in those rites. Plus, he suggested that it would not be wise to piss off my future Mother-in-Law by destroying her baby boy's chance at entry into heaven. I readily agreed.

So, as a family, we attended church every Sunday at St.George's Greek Orthodox Church in Piscataway, NJ. And every Sunday, we had coffee with his parents and siblings and extended relations. My children grew up in this beautiful community, but as a result, they had only a passing knowledge of their Celtic heritage and background.

But now that I had scientific proof of my 100% Irishness, I was excited that my children were a full 50% Irish. In an attempt to encourage interest in their Celtic origins, I asked that one of them submit DNA to see for themselves... were they 50 % Irish and 50% Greek? My strong and brave daughter agreed.

What a SHOCK when the results came back: 50% Irish, 26% Italian, 8% Cretan, 12% Cypriot, 4% Mixed Baltic.

ITALIAN? That did it - enough of the Baklava and Spanakopita, I was going full speed on Soda bread, scones and Irish Whiskey.

Re-enactment of the Irish Brigade, facing Picketts Charge at Gettysburg. 1864

4: IRISH GRANDMA MAGIC

Four years after the divorce, my two oldest children were married, and each of them had one child. I was ready to retire and babysit. But before I could do that, I had to go to Ireland, solve the mystery of Why Mom Left, and have my children come to me there and meet all of their relatives.

My plan was to sell the house, eliminate all debt, put some furnishings into storage and go to Ireland for 6 to 9 months. I have Irish citizenship through my parents, and I could remain in the country indefinitely with my Irish passport. I would purchase a used car, and live in Airbnbs throughout Ireland, my cousins and my children could join me at any time, and they would have free housing, food and transportation with me. Sounded good.

Retiring from nursing after 46 years, I put my 4-bedroom Colonial house, with an acre of land up For Sale.

Would it sell?? How long would it take?? Would I get enough money??

My credit card debt was in the area of $200,000. I had no savings. I received no alimony.

I had investments made up of my half of our financial worth at the time of divorce. The investments were stocks and an annuity. The annuity would not be touched until I needed it for a nursing home. The stocks are what I would live on during retirement because my government pension would not cover my living expenses day-to-day.

FINDING GLOCCA MORA

I could not afford to live an independent life in the Tri-State area (where my children and grandchildren lived) without taking monies every month from my stock investments to pay bills. Should I want to give gifts at Christmas or for birthdays, baptisms, etc, that would involve additional money from my stockpile. If that stockpile had a vacillating annual value (dependent on the stock market's ups and downs), let's say an average of $150,000, and I withdrew $1500 monthly to pay my bills... I would have spent it all in 8 years.

I looked into my future and saw myself as a financial burden to my children. Suddenly the longevity I had been grateful to inherit became a problem, and I was terrified. Contemplating this over one winter weekend actually caused a brief mental shutdown and put me in the hospital. Several diagnoses were put forward: Stroke, TIA, and the onset of Alzheimer's.

The final diagnosis was Transient Global Amnesia brought on by severe emotional stress. It wasn't common, but it wasn't entirely rare, and there was no likelihood of re-occurrence. My children gathered around me and counseled me against any sort of independent travel.

"But Mom, what will happen if you wander around Dublin and can't remember who you are or why you are there? Or even where you are?? You cannot be out of the country; this could happen again. How will anyone know to contact us? We have never met ANY of those people; we don't know them, and they don't know us."

"Exactly!" I responded. "That's why I am going. You need to get to know these relatives who are more blood-related to you than all of Dad's family here. Look - Paddington Bear did it, and he was fine. Like him, I promise to pin a note - In Case of Emergency - in my shirt daily. Besides, the doctor said it would not happen again (As long as I don't try to balance my checkbook ... Ha!). That's it. I am going. And I hope each of you will come and visit and learn all about your ancestral heritage and meet your wonderful Irish family."

I went ahead with my plans and hired a realtor, an award-winning name in the area. She knew the business. She was good at it. I could trust her. She said to list my home for $462,000.

What?? The house was appraised at a value of $500,00 at the time of the divorce! I had paid my Ex half of that amount and was reluctant to lose any more money than I had to. I countered with $475,000. She felt we would not get an offer at that asking price, so she countered with $468,000. I just couldn't do it, so I insisted on $472,500 as the lowest I would go. She finally agreed, but with the caveat that if we had no offers in 10 days, the price would drop to $462,000.

The Open House attracted realtor offices and three couples searching for their "forever home". I received an immediate offer of $462,00. My heart sank, but my realtor assured me, "This is a GOOD offer."

The week passed with only two more viewings. Paperwork was being drawn up to consider the first offer. We agreed that if no other offers came in by the weekend, I would accept that first offer for $462,000.

The weekend came and went. There were no more offers. Monday morning, I called to see if that first couple's mortgage would go through.

"Oh, you're not done yet," says she, "I have a couple who wants to walk through the house this morning. The husband was away all week on business."

By lunchtime, we had their offer: a healthy $472,00 !!!

The first couple was informed that a counteroffer had been received and was asked to make their Absolutely BEST offer. They responded with an increase of only $3000, reaching $465,000.

Likewise, the new couple was informed of their competition and was also asked to make their Absolutely BEST offer. God be praised; they came back with $474,500!

It was done. Somehow, my house had sold in eight days - versus eight weeks - and I had received MORE than my asking price. Someone was looking out for me.

Now, I could eliminate ALL of my personal and household debt, retire, and take my dream journey to Ireland. I began to believe that I did indeed have a spirit guide, and it was my grandmother, Ann Walpole-Gildea. And Grandma must have been eager for me to get on with things because everything began to fall into place.

Thinking that it would take 8 to 12 weeks to complete the sale of my house, I anticipated plenty of time to sell off yard tools, snow shovels, bunk beds, blankets and cushions and couches, serving platters and glassware and cooking appliances, books and books and books and books, miscellaneous artwork and posters, bikes, my kayak, children's toys etc. No. Now I had to be out of the house and have it empty and clean for the new owners by month's end.

It was hair-pulling time. I quietly addressed my grandma and asked for her help. I also put my full faith and trust in believing whatever happened would be for the best. Son of a gun. Within a week, people began arriving at my house in response to Facebook Marketplace ads and were carrying away recliners, bar stools, bookcases and carpets. At work, I was introduced to a new nursing supervisor from Nigeria. It seemed she had family moving here and was furnishing a home for them. That weekend, her husband and sons purchased and carried away my leaf blower, snow shovels, dining room set and dishes, patio furniture and miscellaneous items! I had only the furniture I was keeping for retirement - enough for a small apartment I would rent upon returning from Ireland. This was my final hurdle; it needed to be packed, transported and moved into a storage facility.

Naturally, with all this packing, carrying, and moving, I pulled some muscles that hadn't been used in years.

A trip to the Chiropractor was called for.

At the first visit, I explained my current situation to the doctor. While I was scheduling future sessions, the secretary and I chatted away about my exciting plans. On my next visit, the secretary offered me a business card. Her brother had started a new business recently, and I might be interested in speaking with him. I looked at the card,

"C & C, MOVING and TRANSPORT".

This family referral gave me a fair price and recommended a storage facility they worked with and trusted. By month's end, it was done. I said goodbye to the house on the corner where I had raised my children. Pulling out of the driveway, turning left onto Honeysuckle Way, and driving down the hill, I said:

"Thank you, Grandma. Could not have done it without you. I wonder what's next?"

5: GRANDMA TAKES THE LEAD

The year was 1969. Man had walked on the moon, and my sister gave birth to a daughter. This was Ann's first baby and my parents' first grandchild. The only problem was that Mom and Dad were on Fordham Road, in the Bronx, and Ann was with her West Point graduate husband on a US Army base in Crailsheim, Germany.

Mom was both excited and distraught because she so wanted to be there but could not get time off from work. Somehow, she thought a good solution was to send me. Upon hearing of this, I paraphrased from Gone With The Wind saying,

"….but missus….I don't know nuthin 'bout birthin no babies!"

Mom didn't laugh.

I had just finished my first year of nursing at Hunter College – a branch of CUNY – and Bellevue Hospital. My summer plans were all about Orchard Beach, Central Park and Tommy Sullivan – a sophomore at Marist College. Despite many loud, angry and repetitive protestations on my part, I was to be manhandled onto a plane for Germany. My brother John drove the car with me, Mom, Dad, and Mary McHugh squeezed into it. Even Tommy and a family priest friend – James Anthony Canavan, OCM – were at the gate to see me off. This was before there were any security checks. Everyone could walk you to your gate, kiss you goodbye and watch the plane taxi down the runway and take off.

All of the other passengers were on the plane, and I still refused. Funny, how we are raised to be honest with family, but oh so polite with strangers. When a gorgeous Icelandic stewardess came out to see why I hadn't boarded, I immediately followed her rather than appear to have been rude. All the family watched as the plane took off. I think they were just making sure I didn't jump off.

My European vacation had begun. Things did not go well.

The plane stopped in Reykjavik to refuel and then on to Luxembourg. There I boarded a bus to somewhere in Germany - 3 hours away - where I was met by in-laws, who drove me another hour to the army base. I arrived tired, thirsty, hungry and cranky. Ann was very, very pregnant, also very cranky and couldn't care less about my issues. Baby Jennifer was born within a week, adding to the already tense situation.

I mean, Ann and Rich were newly married – one year – and finding their way. Now they had a newborn, plus a teenager to contend with. Plus, I did not get along with my brother-in-law. I was a Vietnam War protestor, living with an army officer. His position was the Caesar approach: My house. My rules.

I was 18 years of age, living in Army OFFICERS BARRACKS, and having meals at the OFFICERS CLUB, where all the OFFICERS were married, with wives and children. All the while, I was surrounded by an entire Army Base of red-blooded American soldiers my own age and single, but who I was FORBIDDEN to fraternize with because they were "enlisted"… not officers. I bristled at this "class" structure. Not surprisingly, I would sneak out often…

It was a terrible, horrible, awful, not good situation, and my sister needed to regain peace. Did I mention that she is very much like my mother?? Her solution to the problem was like Mom's: send me to another country.

I was sent to my Aunt Teresa in County Derry*, Ireland. Oh Joy!! Aunt Teresa never married and had no children of her own, and I was her namesake. That trip was AMAZING. For 3 weeks, I had 7 girl cousins, close in age, to hang out with. Patsy and Dolores lived in Magherafelt, where their Dad, Uncle Leo, had a Fish and Chip shop. Deirdre lived in the town of Moneymore, on the High Street. Marie, Elizabeth, Eileen and Veronica lived on the farm where my Mom was born, in Quilly. There were dances, walks, Spring Hill, the Causeway, ringing the Chapel bell at The Loup, and there was non-stop giggling and laughing. Deep conversations took place, too, about Catholicism and Civil Rights, Stormont, Vietnam, and those lorries filled with British soldiers holding loaded rifles that drove out of the airport on the day I left in August 1969.

The next five decades passed by in a blur made up of graduations, careers, marriages, the births of our babies and the deaths of our parents and of our Aunt Teresa. During those decades, there were perhaps five or six visits made to see us here in the States, along with the odd card and letter, to keep up the relationship. But I never returned.

I wanted to bring my children to the place I had known such joy but my husband would not agree. It was not just Ireland – he refused to travel anywhere with his wife and kids, saying he did too much travel for his job. This was true; he travelled several times to factories in Hong Kong, Australia, Germany, Thailand, and across the USA. But he had no desire to travel anywhere with his family

I swear I have a bit of Gypsy in me because, in the years between 1974 and 1978, I lived and worked in Minneapolis, Philadelphia, Hartford, Baltimore, St.Louis, Pittsburgh and Anchorage. When we were engaged, I arranged for him to spend weekends with me in each location and a full week in Anchorage, Alaska.

Over the course of 32 years, we visited Disney World twice, Canada once, to visit my friend, and Virginia Beach for a week every year to stay with his relatives, for perhaps a total of 15 years. By the time our divorce was finalized, I was so ready to hit the road! But, I digress.

In September 2019, I flew into Dublin and took a bus to Belfast. There I was met by Veronica's daughter, Jennifer and her husband, Roy. They would put me up at their home for two nights.

Once we were loaded into his car, Roy popped a bottle of champagne and filling two flutes for Jennifer and I; he said:

"It has taken you fifty years, Aunt Terry, but you did it. Welcome back to Ireland."

What a way for my journey to begin!

FINDING GLOCCA MORA

From Jennifer's home on the River Bann in Co. Antrim, I went to stay with my cousin Veronica, in Ballyronan, on the shores of Lough Neagh in County Derry. Two weeks later, I left Veronica's cozy cottage and went to stay with Elizabeth in the Loup, Magherafelt, also County Derry.

My cousin Elizabeth lives with her bachelor son, Joe, and I would stay in their spare bedroom until I made B&B arrangements for myself. Elizabeth is retired and is a widow. I am retired and divorced. Veronica is also a widow but young enough to still work part-time. Like most people, they hadn't visited the tourist sites in their own country, and so our plan was to see all of Ireland together.

The first order of business was to buy a used car. Elizabeth asked her brother, Noel, to look into that. Noel worked for the large corporations that maintained the many wind turbines all over Ireland. He also did some mechanics work on the side, and knew a guy with a car to sell. Within six days he called:

"What do you think about a 2015, SKODA OCTAVIA-ESTATE, 4 doors, hatchback, with 7000 miles, stick shift, and diesel engine? Are you interested?"

I was. They wanted £5,000 in cash, and they would service the car and replace worn tires. SOLD!

But I didn't have a bank account to transfer funds and get it in cash. Not a problem: Elizabeth's son-in-law, JackJoe, would allow me to use his small business account to transfer the money.

There were plenty of jokes about my purchase: why did he need cash? Did he look like IRA? This was the perfect type of car for moving guns or bodies...

Maybe two weeks later, as Elizabeth and I sat in her kitchen, JackJoe's car pulled up in front of the glass doors. His wife was driving, he jumped out of the car while she kept the engine revving. Running up to the table, he threw down a brown paper bag filled with £5000 in loose notes, turned and ran out again, and they sped away. Hahaha...we doubled over laughing because they live next door!

For several weeks, my time was spent cautiously driving around the neighborhood, trying to drive on the side of the road opposite from the side my brain kept wanting me to drive on.

Elizabeth's son, Joe, and her brother, Francis took me up Slieve Gallion Mountain for a practice drive.

"Sure, you'll have no problem a'tall. No one is up there hiking today." said Joe.

It wasn't people that were the problem. I was on the road, supposed to be two lanes, in **OPPOSITE** directions, with no barriers or railings. I was having difficulty keeping the car in the lane while still avoiding the side of the mountain but not tipping over the cliff.

"Go on now, straight up to the very top, keep going, you're doing grand, isn't she Francis?" said Joe.

Francis only mumbled something about the Holy Family and all the Saints in heaven....."

"Now, at the top, you just stop the car and get out. OK? I will turn this car around for ye, and I will drive it down the mountain. Is that OK wit ye ?? If not, you can just leave me and Francis here…"

It's been three years. I am still working toward my Irish driving license.

Elizabeth is a good driver and really liked the car.
"This is a terrific auto, you've got here. Someone is looking out for you up there. Are you sure you didn't give him more than just the money he asked for?"
"Elizabeth, I know… honest to God, since I left for Ireland, things have been falling into place for me!"
I told her about the psychic and my good fortune with my house sale and moving.

We got to planning our first trip, and I announced it would be to Leitrim. In all of Ireland, Leitrim is low on the list of tourist sites, but I felt compelled. When applying for my Irish passport I wanted to use my father's documents, but could not find his civil birth certificate. Despite three searches online, they said he was not there in the records. I got my passport using Mom's documents. Still…I felt this compulsion to find out why Dad wasn't there and fix it. I realize now this was Grandma Anne.

October 2019 was a beautiful autumn. We drove in bright sunshine across the Ulster landscape of fertile green fields dotted with cows and sheep. We made excellent time down into Enniskillen, and on to the N4 as we drove west. Arriving in Mohill around Noon, we parked in the Market Square and set off to find a place to eat lunch. Oddly, there were no people; the streets were empty, and many shops were closed. On the main Street, St Patrick's church drew our attention as it sat on the crest of the hill, and we missed a gentleman stepping out of a doorway behind us. We jumped. He apologized, and of course, we all laughed. He recommended a pub for our lunch called JOHN JAMES. "Aha," I said to them…" this IS Grandma… John James …that's my two brothers, or it's my Dad and his father."

And in we went.

Giggling and excited to see what would happen next, we tucked into a snug and expectantly asked the waitress if she knew the Gildea family: "No. Never heard of them."

Oh dear.

Well, we would have lunch and then search for the parish priest to see if he knew any of my family and why Dad's birth would not be in any civil records.

With that, the front door opened, and our waitress called out, " Ah, Fr. Murphy!! Is it the stew you're here for?? "he replied: "It is indeed – I'll just sit myself over there, will I?"

Wide-eyed, Veronica says to me, "Well now - Grandma's put him right into your lap", and Elizabeth choked on her drink. Not being known for my diplomacy, I went over to the priest, introduced myself, told my tale, and asked for his help. Smiling, he agreed to help in any way, of course. But would I let him eat his lunch first?? We planned to meet at the priest's house in two hours.

FINDING GLOCCA MORA

Fr. Murphy knew several Gildeas, but none from Corlaskagh, where my Dad's home was. Church records were no longer accepted by governments, not since 911, so he sent us to Carrick on Shannon, where there was an office for all birth records for County Leitrim. It was already late, and the office would be closed by the time we would arrive.

We spent the evening walking along the river, looking at all of the boats. I couldn't believe that I was there, at the Shannon river, that I had heard about in songs and stories, and that I had tried to imagine so often. We stayed at a place called Cryan's and in the morning, made our way over to the office.

The lady behind the desk listened to my story and said there could be several reasons why Dad's documents didn't exist. But first, she wanted to check her records. She looked at a database comprised of all church records that were scanned and recorded following the establishment of the Irish Republic. The problem, she explained, was that, often, the ink wasn't dark enough for the scan, the old handwriting was not legible, and many of the records were simply lost to fire and other disasters. She checked for the years 1909, 1910, and 1911 but found nothing. I thought it was over.

To my surprise, she got up and went to a huge vault behind her desk – as you would see in a major Bank Branch. The three of us were impressed when she entered a code, spun the big wheel and pulled open a door as big as herself! Disappearing into the vault, it was only moments before she emerged with a large, old, black accounting type of book. She smiled at us, and when she laid it down it covered the whole desktop.

This book was more than 100 years old, entirely handwritten, from my father's Barony, or locale, recording every birth. It was worthy of a museum, and we sat in awe. She carefully turned the large and long pages so as not to wrinkle or tear. Again, looking at the years 1909 through 1911, hoping that the record of Dad's birth was there and had just not been picked up by the scan. But no……there was nothing in the book, and so it was returned to the vault for safekeeping.

The room was quiet as the three of us sat there deflated. Locking up the vault and spinning that huge dial, the woman spoke to me:

"Well, it is safe to say your father was indeed born here because it was on his passport when he emigrated. Would you like to record your father's birth?"

I think my mouth did, really, drop open. I know I saw Veronica's mouth drop open. Elizabeth, I'm not so sure of.

"But... my Dad is dead. If he were alive now, he would be 109 years old! How is it possible?" Smiling, she said that she would only need a copy of Dad's Death Certificate, and I could get the necessary forms to record him as being born here in Leitrim, Ireland, at his home place in Corlaskagh.

I kid you not... I no longer saw the room around me; instead, in my mind's eye, I saw a woman in period clothing, smiling and holding a newborn baby that I knew to be my father. The woman was nodding her head at me as if to tell me," Yes…please do this, for me."

I knew it was Grandma.

Smiling and nodding my head, I responded, "Yes, please! Thank you! Can I really do that? I can get Dad's certificate when I go home for Christmas and bring it back here."

I told the cousins what I saw in my mind as we sat having drinks (not Elizabeth – she is a Pioneer and was the designated driver).

"Well," said Veronica, "... there is your answer for why you felt you had to come here first. That's what Grandma wanted. Maybe that's another reason why you were brought here to Ireland."

It was. But certainly not the only reason.

Grandma still had more in store for me.

* Derry is the Anglicized version of the Gaelic word, Doire, meaning Oak. All of the Irish names were changed to phonetic spellings of their Gaelic names, or altered in other ways. Thus, Doire became Londonderry. Those of us who prefer to be Irish, rather than English, have always used the original name, Derry, and never use Londonderry.

6: LESSONS IN IRISH HISTORY

The ultimate goal was for my children and grandchildren to be literate in their Irish history and heritage. To know, in their heart and soul, what they said when they told someone, "I am of Irish descent." And before *they* could do that, *I* had to be able to do it.

Elizabeth and I hit it off immediately, as though no time had passed since my visit in 1969, and the same was true with Veronica. I didn't want to leave and move into an Airbnb – there was so much I wanted to learn from them – and Elizabeth encouraged me to stay with her.

It turned out that I lived with Elizabeth for October, November and December of 2019, and not once did I feel awkward. (Talk about the consummate Hostess!) But it worked. And we were both happy spending days with each other. I imagine the rest of the family was waiting to see when the bubble would burst and what would happen between us because, in retrospect, I realize Elizabeth was taking quite a risk in welcoming me into her home with no established date for checkout. Strangely, I never even considered that. I just "knew" this would be good and right for all of us.

Not a doubt in my mind.

FINDING GLOCCA MORA

With my new Library card for the Magherafelt Library, I would take a practice drive into the town once a week to check out and return books. Perhaps, because I was American, the librarians were not too put off when I only requested books about the Anglo-Irish War for Independence and the Irish Civil War.

Every day, I would open up several books, spread them out on the kitchen table, make copious notes and read excerpts to Elizabeth about the evil doings of the English government and the heroic moves on the part of the Irish Volunteers.

I was shocked to hear that Elizabeth knew nothing about the stuff I was learning. Apparently, it was not taught in Northern Irish schools. Duh... dopey me. Of course not. She was educated in Northern Ireland, a constituent country of the United Kingdom. They had a different version of events.

I created a timeline of Irish history for myself – from 1156 through to 1957. This would allow me to better understand the causes and consequences through the centuries that shaped Ireland and its people. Hopefully, it would allow me to understand the social and political climate my mother lived in.

For current purposes right now, I needn't go back to 1156, but I will begin with:
1850 - End of Famine. Due to deaths and emigration, the Irish language is dying, and Irish identity is damaged.
1860 - Fenian Uprising. The constabulary is granted the title of Royal Irish Constabulary (RIC) for so effectively suppressing the uprising

1870 - Campaign for Home Rule (Self-government for Ireland, within the United Kingdom). England is tired of this 'Irish Problem' as it has other conflicts to deal with: the Anglo-Zulu War, the Anglo-Afghan War, the Franco-Prussian War, etc, and considers letting the Irish deal with their own problems

1886 - Prime Minister Gladstone introduces Bill for Home Rule. Loyalists are angry: the Irish will never rule them.

1893 - Home Rule passes in House of Commons but is vetoed in the House of Lords. Unionists protest in Belfast. Gaelic League was founded to revive the Irish language.

1905 - Ulster Unionist Council is formed (Anti Home Rule) Sinn Fein is formed (Support Home Rule)

1911 - House of Lords loses its Veto Power. It can only delay a Bill for two years, hoping to sway votes.

1912 - Bill for Irish Home Rule passes in House of Commons. The House of Lords vetoes the bill - implementation is delayed for two years. Ulster Solemn League and Covenant were created to block Home Rule 'at any cost'.

1914 - August 4th. Irish Home Rule is passed. Britain declares war on Germany. Implementation of Home Rule is delayed until the war is over.

1916 - The Rising at the GPO. A call for independence, but more so for an Irish nation with its own language and culture, not the language and traditions of its coloniser. (To me, this is at the very heart of the issue. For centuries the Irish people welcomed strangers: the Anglos, Normans, and Danes, and it was said that the strangers became more Irish than the Irish. Families intermarried and were made richer by their diversity.

The British were the only group of people to come to Ireland and NOT embrace it. They sought to destroy everything Irish – mythology, religion, language, food, dress, music, culture, song and dance. Even into the 20th century, Britain seemed confused by the continued resistance of the Irish to be subsumed into British culture. Winston Churchill once remarked, "The only problem with the Irish is that they refuse to be British").

He was dead right.

The Irish people did not support the Rising of 1916. These Irish Volunteers were considered a group of troublemakers who were jeopardising the newly acquired Home Rule. But opinions changed when the British government summarily executed this band of school teachers, poets, philosophers and dreamers for taking a stand. That is when the leaders of the Rising captured the attention of most Irish people. Within two years, the goals of this group, for a return to Irish culture, music, dance, literature and language, would result in an overwhelming majority election of their candidates to guide the new government under Home Rule.

1918 - WWI Armistice is signed. First Irish elections are held for a Home Rule government. Sinn Fein wins a majority of seats. Britain announces a "German Plot" - names more than 70 of the newly elected MPs as conspirators. This is an attempt to maintain control over the new Irish government.

1919 - Remaining Irish MPs meet on January 1st but do not report to Westminster. Instead, they establish the Dail

Eireann in Dublin and adopt the Declaration of Independence and the Constitution from the 1916 Uprising. England calls for another election. Irish Volunteers carry out raids on British institutions and the Royal Irish Constabulary (RIC) to finance and defend their new government.
1920 - Britain declares a "Police Action vs A Criminal Conspiracy". Black and Tans are brought in to augment the RIC.

Without going into much detail, I hope this has illustrated that there were forces within the higher levels of the British government opposed to Ireland being governed by the Irish people. They were willing to allow Home Rule on paper, but when the people of Ireland elected the Sinn Fein representatives (instead of the Irish Parliamentary Party, which had dominated the political landscape while under British rule), a German conspiracy was discovered that just happened to involve almost all of the duly elected members of the Home Rule government. What a coincidence!

The next three years are filled with the Irish waging war against Britain and then a civil war against each other. For many reasons woven deep and tight in centuries of Irish history, the people seeking Irish Independence are 99% Catholic. Those who are the descendants of planted loyalist families are Protestant. They are called unionists, seeking to retain union with England.

These loyalist/unionist families accrued tremendous wealth over the previous three centuries. They wield considerable power in the halls of Westminster. Because of their influence, the British government and the monarchy allowed this group to carve out a nation for themselves from the sovereign land that had been Ireland since before the mists of time.

The new statelet of Northern Ireland did not encompass all of the counties of Ulster. Three counties were NOT included, as each of them had a Catholic majority.

The population of the remaining six counties in Ulster was 64% Protestant and 36% Catholic. No matter what any future election would be about, no matter that it would be conducted democratically, the outcome would ALWAYS be in favour of the Protestant majority.

This type of situation can only foster fear and suspicion. It might explain why the Northern Irish Parliament felt the need to have the Special Powers Act renewed every year until it became a permanent law.

Also known as "The Flogging Act", it enabled the government to "take all such steps and to issue all such orders as may be necessary for preserving the peace and maintaining order." However, with only one political party in the government – the Ulster Unionist party – the act was used almost exclusively against the minority population.

Paragraph 23 allowed for the indefinite internment, without warrant or trial, of "any person whose behaviour is of such a nature as to give reasonable grounds to suspect that he HAS ACTED or IS ACTING or is ABOUT TO ACT in a manner prejudicial to the preservation of the peace or maintenance of order."

A person didn't need to commit a specific act. They had only to be suspected and reported to the police, and they could have been imprisoned, without trial, for an indefinite period of time.

Reading this made me think of the situation in America's deep South in the early 1900s when the **KKK** was King. Governments were manipulated to appear democratic but stacked against the minority population so their needs would never be met and their voices never heard.

Mom may have grown up in beautiful, magical Ireland, but her situation there was similar to that of any African American girl living in the beautiful fields of Alabama in 1929.

'H SON, I LOVED MY NATIVE LAND, WITH ENERGY AND PRIDE
'L A BLIGHT CAME OVER ALL MY CROPS, MY SHEEP AND CATTLE DIED
'Y RENT AND TAXES WERE TO PAY, I COULD NOT THEM REDEEM,
'ND THAT'S THE CRUEL REASON WHY I LEFT OLD SKIBBEREEN.

HAPPIER WERE THE VICTIMS OF THE SWO
THAN THE VICTIMS OF HUNGER
WHO PINED AWAY, STRICKEN BY
WANT OF THE FRUITS OF THE FIELD.

IRELAND'S WORST SINGLE DISASTER, THE GREAT FAMINE, 1845 - 1850, RESULTED IN THE DEATHS OF OVER A MILLION OF IT'S PEOPLE, WITH MORE THAN ANOTHER MILLION CONSIGNED TO THE EMIGRANT SHIP. SKIBBEREEN, EPICENTRE OF THIS HORROR, SUFFERED MORE THAN MOST OTHER PLACES AND HERE, IN THE FAMINE BURIAL PITS OF THIS CEMETERY, WERE PLACED THE COFFINLESS REMAINS OF C. 9,000 VICTIMS, A CHILLING REMINDER OF MAN'S INHUMANITY TO MAN.

GO NDÉANA DIA TRÓCAIRE ORTHU.

They died, starving, while the land yielded bountiful harvests for the Masters who shipped it away for a profit

Footprints in bronze of a woman and a child on Main Street in Carrick, leading to the Workhouse

Injustice leaves poor scars that are easily re-opened to bleed again. Black Taxi Tour, 2021

Black Taxi Tour of Belfast, 2021. 100 years of waiting for a United Ireland

7: WHY MOM LEFT IRELAND

The Special Powers Act was the law my family in the North lived under for 51 years, from 1922 until 1973. It explains why my cousin Joseph, Deirdre's brother, vehemently told me to keep my mouth SHUT, when out on the street in Moneymore. It was one thing to say what you thought inside the home, among family, but not outdoors where anyone could hear and report you to the police as a possible troublemaker.

That was in 1969. A man walked on the moon, but neighbors enjoyed exerting power over other neighbors they perceived as "inferior".

My older brother, Johnny, said that Mom had told a story about a group of Black and Tans coming to the farmhouse. Mom had an older half-brother – her father's first wife died in childbirth. This brother, John, was 5 to 6 years older than Mom and would have been between 15 to 19 years old during the Irish War for Independence, 1919-1920. Mom's family was Catholic, so immediately, it was suspected of holding Republican leanings. Apparently, word had been spread to the Authorities that this brother was suspected of running messages for the IRA. The Black and Tans had come to bring him in. The story goes that he escaped out the high field unharmed, although the men had dropped to their knees and were firing after him. Nothing was ever proven. The war ended.

Nine years later may seem like a long time, but the anger and fear from that episode with the Tans, would last for decades.

In the early summer of 1930, my mother was 18 years of age and had acquired a part-time job in a dry goods shop in Cookstown, County Derry. It was not far from her home on the farm in Quilly, but Cookstown was a Protestant Loyalist stronghold. It still is today and hosts some of the biggest parades of the Orangemen's associations. The shop where Mom worked was a thriving business owned by a loyalist Protestant man and his family and was managed by his wife and daughters. Mom's job was cleaning and moving stock out from the backroom or whatever else they needed her to do. I can hear her telling the story now :

"I was carrying out a bolt of cloth to fill the shelf when a customer called to me"

"Here – girl. Help me." So I went to her, curtsied and asked what she needed"

"There is not enough fabric on this bolt. Have you any more of this in the back?"

Mom says she curtsied again and agreed to go at once and look, which she did.

Moments later, she returned with a full bolt of the requested cloth and was about to show it to the customer when the Mistress of the shop called out to her,

"Mary – leave that at once! My daughter will take over. Come to the backroom."

And so, with another curtsy to the woman, Mom scurried off to the backroom to await further instructions.

The mistress was tall, thin, and imperious. When Mom entered the room, she turned on her, "How DARE you speak to any of my customers! Filthy Irish Papist scum... your place is back here, not in front of the shop. You keep your head down, and if anyone asks for help, you are to get my daughters. Do you hear me? Is that clear? Or you will be looking for a job elsewhere!"

I imagine Mom was shocked at first and ready to apologize. But when she heard "Filthy Irish", I'm guessing something snapped, and Mom replied, " Well then, I will just get a job somewhere else" (and maybe her chin was jutting out... just a wee bit).

Ah, poor Mom, she was impulsive. She had forgotten that ALL of the shops in Cookstown (indeed, all of Derry) were owned by wealthy loyalist Protestants who attended church together, married their children to each other and protected one another from any Republican threat, perceived or otherwise.

In my mind, at this point, the mistress sneers at Mom and gloats, "And do you think that ANYONE in Cookstown will hire you NOW?"

Gulp. Needing a good comeback, Mom blurts, " Well then, I will just go to America!" Pointing her long skinny arm at the shop door, the mistress says, " You can Go now!"

What just happened? She was just trying to do a good job. Why did people have to be so mean? How will she tell her Mum and Da? Her wee bit of money was a big help. She cries, thinking how disappointed her parents will be.

Being disappointed would be the LEAST of their problems.

8: I WISH I WERE BACK HOME IN DERRY

Given the small population and how fast news travels, it would not be long before my grandfather would have been approached by friends asking what his daughter said and WHY she was so bold. Although the farms surrounding Quilly – the homeplace – were owned by Protestant families, they all relied on each other and worked together. I can only imagine that a neighbor attended a meeting of his local UVF and found himself listening to talk and outrage about the Donnellys.

Someone at the meeting would bring up the old story about their son, John, suspected of working with the IRA, and now - imagine a slip of a girl, being so bold. What made her think she could get away with that kind of talk? It was disrespectful. She needed to mind her betters. She needed to be taught a lesson. Maybe the whole family needed to be taught a lesson!

And I think that neighbor would have had a secret chat with my grandfather. He would have warned him that the Royal Ulster Constabulary and their B-Specials could become involved unless something was done so that it was made clear that the girl was punished and would not be a problem any more.

An old woman, who had been a close friend to Mom, told Uncle Henry's wife that Mom spent an evening crying. Telling her that she could never leave home, could never leave her mother, her five baby brothers and her sister, Teresa. Together, they thought maybe her parents would let her go to the South, to the Republic, for a while and return home when it was safe. Supposedly Mom was happy with that idea and went home to speak with her father, only to meet him on the lane, calling to her that he had good news. Just that day, he was able to sell the family cow and could afford her passage on a boat out of Belfast. He had bought her ticket. She would be safe. They would be safe.

I have said it before and say it again: everyone alive at that time is dead. There is no one to ask, "What really happened?".

Coming from my nursing background, I look at a group of symptoms, and if it looks like measles, acts like measles, and happens during an outbreak of measles, and if there is no other data to go on, I am going to treat measles.

So here, looking at the social structure of that time, behaviors that were and were not tolerated, descriptions of the justice system, people's attitudes and fears of each other and the government and outside groups... I keep coming to the same conclusion. My Mother was SENT away. She did not choose to go. In an effort to save her and the entire family from retribution, under the Special Powers Act, my grandparents sacrificed their daughter.

I don't know if it was out of shame or maybe fear, but the story of my mom leaving Ireland did not become part of the family history. The next generation heard a happy story about Auntie Mamie, who lived in America, had four children and worked in a hospital. WHY did Auntie Mamie go to America? Well… LOTS of people went to America. And didn't she work in a hospital? Probably she wanted to study to be a nurse and couldn't do that in Northern Ireland. No matter, wasn't she happy and successful??

I'm sorry. I knew that wasn't the truth. True, Mom did work in a hospital: as a switchboard operator on the night shift. Until the Franciscan nuns who ran the hospital, seeing her potential, trained her in accounting and put her in the Billing Office. EVERYBODY liked Mom: nuns, priests, doctors, nurses, auxiliary staff, and even the patients paying their bills. Years later, in her 80s, she received dialysis three days a week, and all of the staff loved the "little Irish lady with the brogue!" I truly believed my mother was happy, that it was her choice to take a big adventure and come to NYC. It certainly fit her personality to take on challenges.

I couldn't believe it when the cousins told me about one of her visits home. Mom had become ill after a dialysis session in Belfast, and she prayed to be allowed to die in Ireland so she would be buried with her parents and sister. She wanted to be back home, even if it meant it was only in death.

Naturally, I shared my theory with my family in The States. It was a mixed reaction – some reluctant agreement about how Mom always pined for her home, and then the general acceptance that ALL immigrants pine for home and that leaving their home was just the fate of the Irish for centuries. As for sharing my ideas with the family in Ireland, they thought I was a typical American, making something more than it was.

Elizabeth belonged to the Historical Society of The Loup in Magherafelt. She arranged for us to meet with the Director, Sean Corey, so I could tell him my ideas and get his reaction. Sean's first response was that, as awful as it sounds to us today, it was common for families to send daughters away to work as domestics. But alone? Hmm, he hesitated but said it was not out of the question. And not send any other children, especially the boys, as they got older? Well…he explained that each family situation was different. Basically, he and Elizabeth saw it as the classic Irish story: poverty, lack of opportunity, and education led families to send their children off to find a better life away from Ireland.

The conversation went to other topics for a while. Then I asked Sean about the Special Powers Act. I asked for his opinion as to what would happen if a young woman from a Catholic Irish farm family had a job in one of the shops of Cookstown but, when reprimanded by her Mistress, told her the equivalent of "I don't need your stinking job". He laughed as though such a thing would never happen and said, "Oh…she would have to go, for sure! She would be dealt with…"

And there was my answer.

Before I left the United States, I went to my parents' grave, and spoke to my mother: "Mom? I'm going to Derry. Tracy, Elizabeth and Veronica told me what you prayed for. I'm so sorry, Mom. I never knew. I wish I did. I wish I had done something, but I didn't. But what I CAN do now is take some of this soil you're part of and mix it with your parents and your sister, Teresa. Is that OK?" I dug up a cup of dirt, sealed it in a jar, and brought it with me.

When I asked Elizabeth if that would be okay with the family, she suggested I place a plaque on the grave with Mom's name, stating that she is interred in America. All of the Donnellys agreed. That December, as we all gathered at the gravesite for their Mother's anniversary, Mom's plaque was there too and "Auntie Mamie "was remembered by all.

My mothers parish church in Moneymore, Co. Derry and the cemetery beside

Plaque on the Donnelly Family Grave for my Mother to be remembered in Ireland, along with her parents.

The Donnelly Family, Quilly, Co.Derry. L-R: Henry, Gerry, Da, Teresa with Leo, Leonard, Mam, Mary (Mamie), Hugh

Mom's home in Quilly, County Derry

9: IRELAND IS CLOSED FOR BUSINESS

Christmas 2019 was the first one in my daughter's new home and the first for her new baby daughter as well. I flew home for the event, laden with gifts for the family: knitted Irish sweaters, scarves from Donegal, socks from the Book of Kells Collection, Irish Whiskey fudge, Dulaman Gin and Jameson's Whiskey.

Plans were made for family members to fly to Ireland in Springtime and Summer. The expectation was that I would return to the States in late Autumn and commence my search for an apartment. My sister gave me a copy of Dad's Death certificate to bring back to Leitrim so that I could register his birth, and everything seemed to be humming along.

In January, I moved into an Airbnb down in Wicklow, with plans to stay there for three months. Wicklow would be an opportunity to see Glendalough and the Wicklow mountains, travel back up to Dublin for the museums and do the tours of the GPO, Kilmainham Gaol, and Glasnevin Cemetery.

March, April, and May, I would find a place near Leitrim, spend the Springtime where my Dad grew up and maybe research my Grandma and her family.

June, July, and August would be Limerick for the many summer festivals within a 2-hour drive from there, and then wrap it up with a month or two up in Donegal before I traveled back home.

I had my plans made, my houses booked in advance, the car was safe, and I had switched out my American SIM card in my phone for an Irish one. My banking arrangements were all humming along, and so I was ready.

What could POSSIBLY go wrong??

The cousins - affectionately referred to by now as the Derry Girls - came for a visit in February. Almost all of the conversation was about this outbreak of another SARS-type virus in Italy and whether the football match in Dublin between Ireland and Italy would be allowed to take place. It seemed to happen simultaneously that while hundreds of Italian fans were flooding Dublin city, alongside hundreds of Irish fans, the World Health Organization announced it was not an outbreak but a GLOBAL PANDEMIC.

Pandemic?

Like 1918? The Spanish flu? Millions of people dead? Like the stuff of blockbuster movies... Biblical proportions?

I didn't believe it. So I called my son, a nurse educator because I was sure he would have access to the latest updates from the CDC and etc.

"Bill - what is all this hype? Is it mostly media seeking high ratings? What do you see in the ER?"

Bill likes to joke, but in a dead flat serious voice, he said,

"Mom - it's bad. They can't get a handle on this virus. It acts like a flu in lots of people, but it's different in others. This bug seems to be able to mutate and change rapidly. We can't pin it down. This is for real."

A killer bug? Back home? With my kids in the middle of it? Oh, hell no. I need to be with them.

"Okay, Bill, I'm booking a flight home tomorrow, or as soon as I can get there."

Bill was adamant, "NO! You can't go anywhere. Yes, you're healthy and strong and all that, but Mom, your immune system is close to 70 years old. NO. And if you did come back, knowing you and knowing the current shortage, you would be sucked right back into work on the wards. Where you will most likely get it and then die... alone, in isolation. STAY WHERE YOU ARE."

I was shocked, but I knew he was right.

I lived through lockdown from January 4th to May 30th at my B&B - Minmore Mews. It was a beautiful setting of one-story stone buildings. Part of the Coolatin Estate, it had been the land agent's domain from the time of the famine. Each building had been restored into an apartment but bore its original name; the Byre, the Coach House, the Stables, etc.

There were two other residents there. Mary had the apartment beside mine, and John was across the courtyard. Not allowed to travel more than 5km from home, we went for walks and often saw each other from our windows. Mary was a retired nurse too, from England, who had come to visit family. John was a genealogist who frequently traveled to Dublin for his research. Conversations were only possible when we were outdoors and when the weather permitted. So - they were short.

I was irritable and itching to do SOMETHING. My entire being was prepped and ready to GO... to DO, SEE... to EXPLORE... to DISCOVER. But no... all of Ireland was shut down.

So I signed up for an online dating site.

I would meet Irish men my age who had never heard my jokes or stories, and I would hear theirs. Plus, with video, it would be a proper chat, and we could each have our own pot of tea or a drink!

I was shocked to discover how many Irish men are not scintillating conversationalists. All one-word answers. I was pulling hen's teeth and getting tired of it. But then, Michael responded to my message.

Michael is a true Irish GEM - a quick wit, intelligent conversation, interested in American politics and able to teach me a bit about Irish politics; compassionate and a gentleman. We hit it off from the start, and for an entire year, we would have a video chat every evening before bed.

My next rental was booked in County Clare. It sat on the border with Limerick. Was it luck, or was it Grandma: Michael lived in Limerick! As it turned out, his home was less than 12 km from my location. This meant we could actually spend time together when the lockdown lifted. I had a lot to look forward to!

May 30th, I said goodbye to my friends at Minmore Mews and moved into Cratloe Woods Lodge. My hostess was so tickled to learn that I had found myself an Irish "beau" that she had the sitting room set up with a bottle of wine, two glasses and candles. I laughed, " What a Romantic".

Michael finally met me the next evening, although we felt like old friends. His arms were full; a dozen red roses, a bottle of wine, and an apple tart! I was stunned and so very pleased and surprised; this was unexpected. But not as much of a surprise as when he put his arms around me - as I was placing the roses into a vase - and planted a long kiss on my mouth.

My brain screamed,

"How dare he??? Who does he think I am ???"

But another part of my brain and my anatomy shouted: "I remember this!"

And there was also a voice in my head, saying, "You are turning 70 soon - this may never happen again - GO for it!"

I responded wholeheartedly, and we laughed all evening at how amazing it was for us to be acting like two teenagers. And also, how lovely it was too.

As I crawled into my bed that night, I had another chat with Grandma Ann:

"Grandma... you are the real deal. Thank you for keeping me safe and for putting happiness into my life."

Michael had part-time work commitments, but we went for a drive at least once a week, and he gave me recommendations for sites to visit. I told him about registering Dad's birth and that I needed to go to Leitrim for two days. My plan was to stay at Cryan's again, but Michael insisted I go to the Bush Hotel. It was where he would stay when he traveled. I was hesitant, but he insisted, and he made the booking.

While driving there, I passed a turf field being cut and laid out to dry. Dad had told us stories about this, so I stopped to take pictures. A man engaged me in conversation, and, as you do, I told him the family name and that I was looking for the homeplace. "Well now..." says he, "I recently sold some cattle to a man by that name. I have his number here. Will I give it to you? But, uh, well, I must say he is a bit of an odd duck. Now, don't get me wrong, he is fierce smart! But he won't pay his taxes, and I think he lives in the woods..."

This was too good to pass up. In addition to looking for information about my grandmother's family, my brother reminded me that we had a first cousin living in Carrick on Shannon, who had returned to Ireland when he retired. Thomas Joseph was the son of my aunt Bea, born in the 1930s. He would be up in years now if he were still alive. Everyone in the family lost touch with him when he moved out of his apartment and into what we thought was a type of assisted living. So I took this "odd Duck" phone number, laughingly saying that he could well be in my family.

The Bush Hotel was an Old Madam - 220 years on the same site, serving people on their travels. It had such an Old World feeling and all the staff were glad to meet you. Although I told them I was looking for family named Gildea, no one seemed to have any information.

After an Irish breakfast (that would carry me through to the night!) I called the phone number and spoke to the man who answered. He repeated everything I said to him, "You're American? Born in New York, and your father was James Gildea? And he had a sister Annie and a brother Joseph?"

"Yep... that's me," I said, trying to move things along.

After a long pause, he said, "Well, now, I am your first cousin as my father is Joseph Gildea, with a sister Annie and a brother James in America. And what's your name ??"

Holy Moly! I might never have found him if I hadn't stopped in the turf field. We agreed to meet at the cemetery in Mohill, at our grandparents' grave. Sitting in my car - it started to rain - we talked for two hours. He didn't recall who the man was that gave me his number and reflected that he never goes to Roscommon to buy cattle. However, he was offered a good deal in May, which was the only time he made a purchase. When I asked if he knew anything about our cousin Thomas, he responded, "Do you know the Bush Hotel?"

(What?? That's where Michael sent me! Or was it Grandma?)

"Well, go in there and ask for the chef, Hughie. Thomas Joseph is nearly 90 years of age, and Hughie is his carer. The council gave him a wee house up Summer Hill, in Carrick on Shannon."

That evening, as I ordered my dinner, I asked the waitress if there was a chef named Hughie and explained why I wanted to meet him.

"Ah, he will be delighted to meet you. I'll tell him, and he will be out to you after you have your meal. Why didn't you tell us you were looking for Tommy Doherty? We all know Tommy; Hughie's been caring for him these past few years."

Hughie joined me for my dessert, and we had a great chat. A plan was made to meet in two days, and Hugh would take me to Tommy's place. The next day, I planned to drive to Ballinamore and hand in the documents and application to register Dad's birth.

None of this trip would have been possible without the GPS on my phone! I could go anywhere so long as my phone was charged. Off I went, through the town, past some townhouses, following signs for Ballinamore. At one "T" junction, I had a choice: Ballinamore to the right and Foxfield RC. Church, to the left.

A strange name for a Catholic church, I thought. Then it came to me: That's the church where Grandma Ann got married! Ballinamore would wait for another day. I made a sharp turn to my left.

Parked at the church and walking around looking like a tourist, I drew the attention of the only woman there.

" Can I help you?"

" Oh, Hi. Yes, please - do you know how old the church is?"

" Well, the year on the stone says 1830, I think."

" Ahh, great! This is the altar where my grandparents married!"

" Isn't that lovely... and who are they?!

" Well... it was back in 1904, hahah... Ann Walpole and John Gildea."

"Walpole and Gildea, is it?" and she gets a big smile, as if she knew them and her younger than me. "So you're here visiting Frank, are you? "

FRANK? Frank Who?

Seeing my puzzled expression, she goes on,

"He would be your cousin... on both sides of the bed, as we say! His grandparents are Ellen Walpole and Francis Gildea. Also married here that same year. Ann and Ellen were two sisters who married two brothers, John and Francis Gildea. Do you not know him??"

She gave me directions, my GPS found his house, and I left a note in his mailbox with my phone number. When I was back at the Bush Hotel, he called me, and we made plans to meet on Sunday before I drove back to Limerick.

Talk about " Serendipity". This was a bit much. Only here for one week and without the services of any directory, with no locals knowing any of my family, and yet I find and meet two first cousins and a previously unknown 2nd cousin. And all because a man was cutting turf, and I stopped to watch. This had to be Grandma Ann's doing!

Minmore Mews, County Wicklow at sunrise, March 2020

Spiritual Maze at Glendalough, Co. Wicklow

My rental near Limerick - ready to meet my Beau!

10: A SAFE LANDING

No one expected there would be a vaccine for another six to eighteen months. I couldn't afford to continue to pay for B&B locations. I needed to get an apartment.

Just the thought of that made my brain fuzzy: finding and moving into temporary housing was something you did in college. NOT as you were preparing to celebrate your 70th birthday. Still, it had to happen.

OK. But where? At first, I considered the North to be near my cousins. But BREXIT was about to happen, and I had recently insured my car in the Republic. Who knew what type of regulations or restrictions would be put in place. No, better to stay in the South.

Galway? Kerry? I could go anywhere... I could stay in Limerick, and Michael was there, to be sure.

I was mulling it over when I had a realization: none of these counties holds any meaning for me. My Ireland was Derry and Leitrim. I had an opportunity to live for an entire year in the place where my Gildea ancestors lived, where my grandmother was raised and married, and where my father called home. That was it. I would find a place in Leitrim, in Carrick on Shannon.

With an online app, I was able to view available listings, and I made a list. In late August, I booked myself into the Bush Hotel to conduct my search.

UNBELIEVABLE:

"Oh no, sorry, Miss. That listing is not available. None of them are. There is not one property to let in all of Carrick. I know it's shameful the website has not been updated, but what can we do? We have no staff to do it, what with the Pandemic, and it's all we can manage to keep the office open, so it is! The problem is that anyone with a rental place will only let it for weekends or holidays, which pays more money than a long-term let, such as you're looking for. I'm sorry now, but best of luck to you."

Back at the hotel, I shared my woes with the staff members I had come to know. One woman, Rosie, asked me what it was, exactly, that I needed, as she might know someone.

I checked out the next morning, which was a stunning summer day, especially for Ireland. Looking forward to a beautiful drive back to Limerick, I suddenly thought: the day would be over when I returned to the Lodge. Why not sit in the sun for a bit and enjoy it? There were roses in the garden alongside the car park, so I dragged my suitcase over and perched on the stone wall.

Not ten minutes had passed when a gentleman approached me. Had I NOT stopped for a sit-down, I would have pulled out of the car park, driven through town and been over the bridge into Roscommon.

"Are you the woman looking for an apartment?"

"I don't know if I'm the woman you're looking for..." I stammered, "... but I am looking for an apartment."

"I'm Joe Dolan. I own the Bush Hotel, and my wife Rosie told me about you. I might have something you would be interested in. Ah, but you've checked out already..."

" Not a problem," I blurted out, " I am in no hurry, and not going anywhere."

" Well then, will you meet me in the lobby at 2 pm, and I can show you what I have?"

"Yes, sir! I'll be there."

Putting my luggage into the car, I went to the church across the street, lit a candle and prayed, "Thank you for Rosie!"

Then I sat eating ice cream in front of Mulvey's Stationery, next door to the hotel.

At 2 pm, Joe Dolan took me to a Victorian red door entrance between Mulvey's and the hotel, and we went in. At the top of the stairs was a door with two stained glass panels, and up another half staircase, there were two large bedrooms, fully furnished as hotel guest rooms. A small office looked out on Main Street, and The Poitin Still, just across the way, as did an adjoining sitting room.

Stepping into the sitting room was like stepping back in time to the early 1900s, with two golden upholstered wingback chairs flanking a table with a Tiffany-style lamp and an open fireplace (but with an electric heater). The kitchen had a very tall window (4 1/2 feet) that let in lots of sunlight and looked out the back to the hotel dining room.

"Well, what do you think?" asked Joe.

"I love it! I'll take it! How much? Never mind, I don't care!"

We both laughed and negotiated a price beneficial to each of us. I would move in September 1st.

Anybody I spoke to in Carrick on Shannon did not believe my story. It was assumed that I was a relative of Joe and Rosie Dolan because no one could find a rental. Unless you had supernatural powers, and while I didn't have powers, I certainly had a connection!

Every evening news show reported the daily death rate. Lockdown restrictions were determined in accordance with whether the virus was spreading or being maintained at a manageable rate for the hospitals. That summer, all restaurants and pubs were closed for indoor service. In true entrepreneurial fashion, outdoor seating became the norm across all of Ireland - despite its famous rainy weather - and summer travel could continue. Skellig Michael had been on my wish list for years. The Derry girls came to me in Carrick, and we travelled the Ring of Kerry, took a boat tour out to the Skelligs, spent a night in Dingle and traveled back to my place. Needless to say, they were impressed with my new abode and agreed that this was not just "Luck".

My grandmother, Ann, was truly looking out for me.

Shopping remained limited, so the outdoor car boot sales provided entertainment. There I met a lovely, considerate guy from Dublin, Warren, in his fifties, with a **WICKED** sense of humor. He had recently moved to Leitrim too, and we became best buddies. Soon, Warren introduced me to other people he met, and a social circle began to develop. The weekly Farmers Market in Carrick meets every Thursday, and our little group would show up for the craic. It was an hour or two of discussing conspiracies, government stupidity, sharing news in general and slagging each other in good fun. I was christened a "dozey bastard!" when I failed to pay attention and walked past the chip shop we were going to for lunch. Haha! I loved it!

There was Frankie, early 60s, another Dub, covered in tattoos, affectionately referred to as "The Bastard", who lives alone on his land in Aughnasheelin with a pet pig, named Josephine, four dogs, numerous chickens and their Cock, and his beautiful traveler pony named Gypsy. Frankie's wife doesn't prefer country life, so Rita remains in Dublin, near the kids and grandkids, and travels out to Leitrim several times a month.

Two years older than me, Matty is a no nonsense guy: "Shut yer mouth and just do it. What are ye yapping about?"

Matty retired from decades of construction work in Dublin, was widowed, took a trip to Thailand and met Jida – 26 years his junior. But Love is blind, and after a ceremony in Thailand, she came to Ireland with him and married him again, here in Carrick on Shannon.

Peter lives in an apartment upstairs from Matty and Jida. Also from Dublin, he has a very dry sense of humor, and spends his time writing plays – all of which he submits to contests, and a few of which awarded him prizes. With a varied work background and growing up as a city kid, Peter is a realist. Or, some might say, a pessimist. Peter's quote is, "Ach, it will all end in tears..."

Mary raises and trains champion Irish wolfhounds. Due to Lockdown, she was unable to socialize a new pup named

Falcon. We met Mary at the Farmers Market, sitting there, calmly introducing Falcon to this small crowd of humans. Poor Falcon would shiver while her brother Bran, another champion, was posing for selfies with marketgoers. The dogs were magnificent, and Mary enjoyed our little group.

And, of course, I had all the staff at the hotel looking out for me now that I was a sort of permanent hotel resident. Joe made it clear that I was to call the front desk if there were any problems and his maintenance staff would be over to fix it.

I was in a safe, comfortable place with friends and neighbors looking out for me. Michael had come for a weekend visit, and we continued video chatting every night. He was a godsend during the American presidential elections in November because I could not get American News on my hotel TV channels. Michael had CNN via satellite dish. He would call me, then turn his tablet camera around to face his TV so we could watch it together!

December was icy, and the death rates were erratic. I went to Derry for Christmas, but a new Lockdown was announced suddenly, to begin at midnight, Boxing Day, cutting short the planned visit.

January was nothing but frigid. How is it possible that the temperatures here are not as low as in New England, but it feels so much worse? It is NOT a "dry" cold, like Minnesota. This here is damp and wet and seeps into your bones. The only cure is a hot whiskey in front of an open fire. I know it's true because I have tried it.

Michael had knee surgery in January. His daughter moved in with him. Abruptly, our video chats came to an end. I signed up for another online dating site.

A visit from Mary's champions - Falcon and Bran. They don't fit in my apartment!

A cast of characters - Warren, Myself, Matty, and Peter

The red door to my apartment, Main Street, Carrick on Shannon. Bush Hotel is on the Left.

Rainbow over the Shannon River, at Boardwalk in Carrick on Shannon

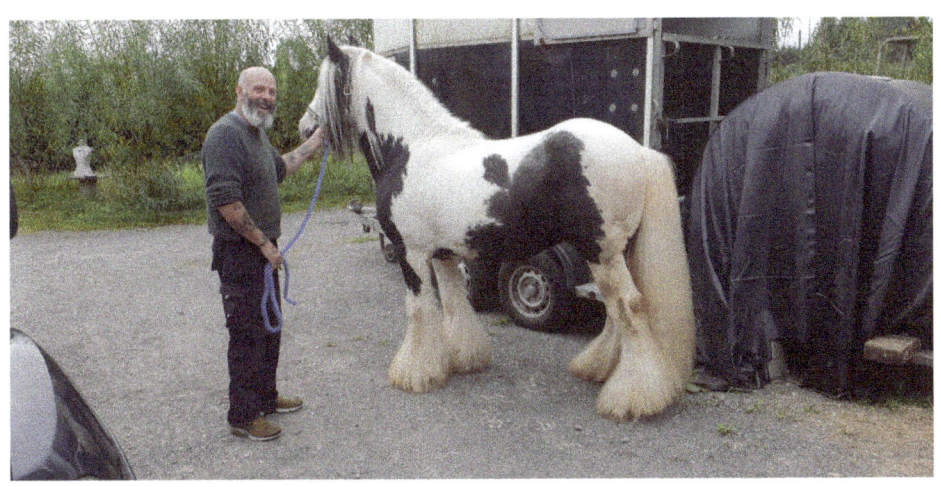

Frankie and his Gypsy

Skellig Michael, seen from our tour boat. It was Veronica that pulled me to the side of the boat for my first view of it

11: SHOULD I STAY OR SHOULD I GO?

January, February, March, and April were uneventful. Uneventful as far as this story is concerned. There is another story, to be told another time, about how truly ODD that "odd duck" relative turned out to be. A gypsy curse was involved, and it looks to be coming true, but, as I say, another story for another day.

May arrived and brought the Derry girls once again. This time we drove the length of Ireland's Eastern coast. Beginning in Dublin, we made our way to Wicklow, New Ross, Waterford, Ardmore, Cobh (known as the 'Harbor of Tears' - the port where my father boarded the ship to America), Kinsale, Skibbereen, and down to Mizen Head. The trip back took us to Beal na Blath, Cork City, Kilkenny and Meath. In Meath, we celebrated Bealtaine on the Hill of Uisneach, with a large bonfire at sunset, fire dancers, and players dressed as Druids and Fairy Folk. I was finally getting to check off items on my Ireland To Do and See List, which got me thinking about when I would return to the States.

By now, I had been living in an apartment and paying all the usual bills for nine months. I canceled my MediCare since I couldn't use it while I was here for two years. It was costing me almost $300 per month out of my pension. I now had Irish health insurance and car insurance. I had gone through a winter of paying for heat and electricity and all the internet I could stream live during COVID. I had an Irish SIM card in my phone. My prescriptions were handled by my doctor, my eyeglasses had been replaced by a local optometrist and my abscessed tooth had been cared for by a local dentist. Because I had packed for only two seasons and a maximum of nine months away, by now, I had purchased a new wardrobe as well.

I worked through my budget, remembering how frightened I had been two years earlier about whether I could find affordable housing, etc, in the Tri-State area. As I suspected, the numbers showed that I was financially better off living here in Ireland.

As a pensioner over the age of 65, I was entitled to free doctor visits, as well as free transportation on any public bus or railway anywhere in the country. As a pensioner, my heating bill was subsidized by the government. My monthly prescriptions were now costing me 1/3 of what I had paid in the States. My apartment was in the center of town, had free parking, which was lit up at night and safe, and was within walking distance of church, library, grocer and gift shops. The price of clothing or groceries was not any worse than what I paid back in New Jersey. Bottom line, I had money left over at the end of every month.

Could I really give up my life in the United States? I had spent my whole life there; I had lived on the East Coast and out in the Mid-West, as well as visited 30 out of the 50 states. Why didn't I feel homesick? Could it be memories of prior lives lived in Ireland or just the fact that every home I visit here feels like the home I had with my Mom and Dad? I put off any decisions until they were necessary and prayed for a clear sign of my direction.

Meanwhile, the dating site was fun this time.

I met a Scotsman living in Mayo who had lived and worked in France for 25 years until his wife died. He had a totally weird accent.

I met a man from the North who works as a Theatre Adjudicator. I had never heard of such a thing. The Irish seem to take their playwrights and theatre very seriously, with most towns having an acting troupe. Annually, they have regional "play-offs", if you will, and he sits as a judge. Fascinating guy.

There was an insurance broker from Galway who knew way too many statistics for normal conversation, much less anything approaching romance, and two musicians from Dublin who could never get away from the city.

Finally, there was George. Born in Northumbria, he had a career in the UK, spent summers in Ireland and was sympathetic to the Irish cause. What can I say? I was enamored with his emails even before we met. In person, he was warm, embracing, and fun. At that first weekend, he made me feel protected and cherished, feelings I had missed out on for many years.

I tried to find reasons for it NOT to work since I didn't know my future after the next year, but we couldn't help it. Every time we got together, it felt more natural, like we were old lovers but new friends.

At the same time, I met a young woman from Spain who came to Ireland to become fluent in spoken English. The problem was that she couldn't understand the Irish, speaking English! She found my American accent much easier to work with, and so we met several times to share a pot of tea and conversation.

She was looking for housing in Ireland, hopefully, to share a house with two other women. As I helped her with this, I learned that three women could pay 300 Euro each per month and have the use of a house with a garden. I was paying 780 Euro per month for a walk-up apartment.

If I rented a house and then rented a room to this young woman, or any other young woman, I could make money on the deal!

George thought it was a good idea but took it a step further: I should buy a house.

NO. I was adamant. I was too old to be worrying about another house, worrying about maintaining property. If I rent, all the headaches go to my landlord. A house in Europe would be an albatross around my children's necks, trying to sell it after I died.

George didn't change his mind, nor did he argue with me. We looked at rental properties, and I decided on an adorable cottage on a cul de sac overlooking the Shannon. I left my number with the listing agent to schedule an interview with the owners.

Driving home, George asked to stop by a house for sale that he found very interesting. "Sure," I said. "Look all you want. I found what I was looking for. But if it will make you happy, and satisfy your curiosity, let's go!"

We drove to an area in Carrick that I had never found appealing. It was attached townhouses, three stories high. Very unusual, almost all housing was no more than two stories. Cream-colored pebble dash with a black tarmac parking area. "Are you joking me?", I began, "I can't buy something like this and send a picture home to America! Where is the small cottage? The thatch? The rose bush and shamrocks??" and we both laughed. George was curious and continued to walk about the area, while I enjoyed the last of the sunlight, leaning against the car. Behind me, I heard a truck pull up. A window rolled down, and a voice asked, "Do you need any help?" As I pushed off the car, I said, "No, thank you. My friend here is just curious...." turning to face the stranger, I saw the sign on the side of his truck. It said: MAGHERAFELT Tyres.

My mother was born in Magherafelt, County Derry. Surprised, I approached the driver and began teasing him, "What are you doing down here in the South? That's a Northern Irish truck you have there."

Hearing my American accent, he smiled and came back at me, "Sure – what would YOU know about that?"

By now, I was right beside him and explained about my mom and the cousins and asked why he was so far from home. "These are my buildings," he said. " I'm selling them. Come on – I'll take you in and show you! My name is Cathal Quinn, by the way,"

Before I could protest, George was beside me asking questions. In we went, and introductions were made.

FINDING GLOCCA MORA

To make this long story short, let me say that the inside was new and surprisingly spacious. A patio garden on the second floor took my breath away. The ground floor was a separate "granny flat" – kitchen, bedroom, bath – which would be perfect for the Derry girls when they would visit or for the family from the States. I saw potential everywhere. Ah, but what was the asking price? I had seen other listings in the area, and nothing was cheap.

Surprise. It was in my price range...

George and I took the listing agent's name and returned the next day. None of the appeal had been lost. We considered every option, every risk, every potential flaw. What if I hated it? What if I moved back to NJ in 2 years? Did it require upfront repairs? No matter what we came up with, it would pay for itself, it would more likely increase in value, and I could just enjoy it until I didn't any more.

We both looked at each other. What was happening here? How did it turn out this way when I was SO Against purchasing a house? How did I get to this point?

This would never have happened if that truck didn't appear with the name MAGHERAFELT painted on its side. As it turned out, the truck had been sold as used, and Cathal had never bothered to remove the painted signage. If he had, I would not have engaged him in conversation. Grandma? ?????

George had his own house on the Wild Atlantic Way, farther south. This house would be my own home, bought with my own money. Plus, I could earn some money if I did a few weekend rentals. With that and the money I saved by living in Ireland, I could easily afford a trip home yearly.

My children and grandchildren could visit Ireland and all of Europe over the coming years and have a home on this side of the Atlantic.

It looked like Grandma wanted to bring future generations of her descendants back to their homeplace, in Leitrim.

I wasn't confident one way or the other. If I made an offer and got the house, that would be the adventure of a lifetime. It wasn't meant to be if I didn't get the house. If I didn't make an offer... I would never know, and that would bug me forever. Simple: Go for it.

So I made a cash offer. Later that afternoon, I received a phone call, "Ms Gildea? Congratulations, you have bought yourself a home."

Touring Ireland with my 'Derry Girls' - this is a lake in Donegal

A wintry drive in Wicklow

Celebrating the Goddess, Eriu, at Bealtaine, on the Hill of Uisneach

Cathal's truck that made me stop and speak with him, that led to looking at the house, that led to buying the house!

12: ARRIVAL

Hard to believe that I have lived here for one year now. Of course, with so much to do, time flies.

The Derry girls showed up with curtains, a tea kettle and toaster, and Gin glasses. No grass grows under those dancing feet!

Matty and Jida were a huge help hanging drapes and mirrors and organizing the kitchen, among many other jobs.

Frankie and Rita helped to organize the first party, when my son visited with his family, and had a cake made saying, "Welcome to Ireland".

Peter held up a glass and admitted he was wrong when I bought the house and had said, "Ach now, it will all end in tears..."

There is still so much I want to do and see, especially research on Grandma's family, the Walpoles. It is an unusual Irish name and only appears in records, I am told, for a period of maybe 250 years.

The story I alluded to about my "odd duck" relative must also be finished. It involves researching the farmland my Dad's family owned and whether I can purchase a small portion of it.

I have to believe that George is also a gift from Grandma. He has been invaluable in many ways, helping me with the house and the garden. And, of course, I never would have the house if he hadn't found it in the first place!

We were recently discussing all of this and my book project, and I think George has summed it up well:

"Terry, you have been on an interesting journey. You have met lots of people that you connected with along the way. Some of these people, you re-connected with, some you met for the first time. Some are still with us, and some are long dead. The journey and the people have enabled you to fully return to this 'home left behind'.

You are no longer part of that widespread Irish Diaspora... you are returned home. You are living in the same parish as your forefathers and have fully integrated into your Irish family as it is today. Part of the culture those forefathers would still recognise."

He's right. I have. And hopefully, this journey will continue for me for another decade or a bit more. During that time, my grandchildren, who are also part Peruvian, Italian and German, will visit often and embrace Ireland as a home. For hasn't this magical island welcomed strangers for centuries? So that "the strangers became more Irish than the people themselves."

Just as Grandma Ann brought me home, I can now bring my own descendants "home".

From Derry in the North, to the southernmost tip of Ireland - Mizen Head, County Cork!

Lismore one of the many castles built by strangers who came to Ireland only to become Irish themselves

Viking display in Waterford; but I have no Viking DNA....

Leitrim landscape, seen from the top of Sheemore

A lovely flock just outside of Galway

Making friends at Sean's bar in Athlone - just passed final exams!

The Cousins, in Donegal. November 2019 L-R AnneMarie, Eileen, Elizabeth, Marie and Veronica

Dad's abandoned home. I will pick the rushes for Brigid's crosses from these fields and send them back to family

I'm here to stay. Do come for a visit SLAINTE!

Story Terrace

www.ingramcontent.com/pod-product-compliance
Lightning Source LLC
Chambersburg PA
CBHW042128100526
44587CB00026B/4210